Legless In Dubai

A novella by Kara Clarke

KARA CLARKE

Cover design by Createspace
Cover Photograph © Kara Clarke
ISBN-13: 978-1499357349
ISBN-10: 1499357346

CONTENTS

PREFACE

On the whole, this is a true account of my experiences in the United Arab Emirates, though the names have been changed to protect the guilty. If your experiences are different, you probably didn't stay with Legion. Dubai is a city of divergence; where great wealth flaunts itself in the face of great poverty, where a single woman can be imprisoned for sharing accommodation with a man, and yet prostitution is rife, where foreign workers are exploited and treated as slaves while their masters lounge in decadent luxury. Don't be fooled by the humour of my account; this is a scary place for a woman travelling alone.

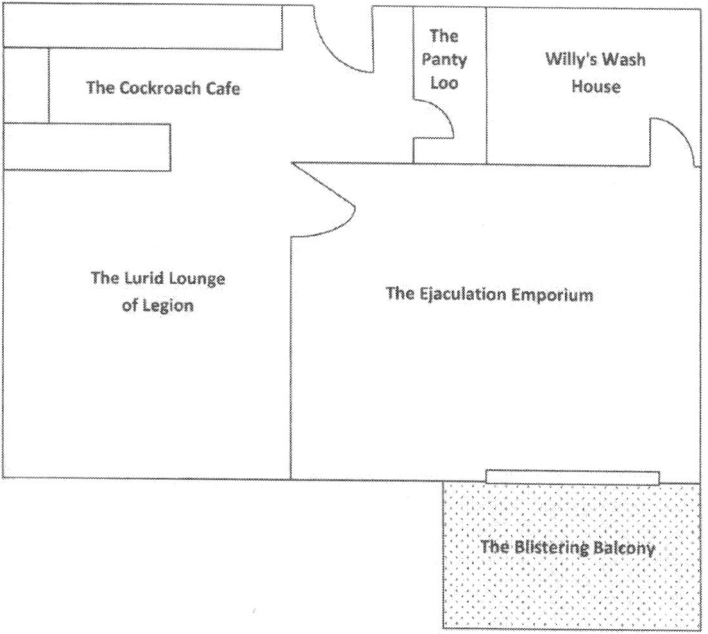

The Floor Plan of Leg's Dubai Apartment

Leg had gone and wasn't coming back.
He'd left me, confined and Legless in his
Dubai apartment, knowing that if the
authorities discovered me, I wouldn't have
a Leg to stand on.

CHAPTER 1: The Invitation

On the 8th November 2011 I took a long, hard look in the mirror. The last twenty years were beginning to take their toll. The life I thought would go on forever, was already nearing the finish line. Time was running out. My good friend and neighbour was only one of a whole bunch of friends and family struggling with cancer. Some had already succumbed, some were still fighting, and I knew many more were waiting on the horizon. It made me reflect on my own life. Divorced for almost twenty five years, the last seven without a man in my life. It's a long time. Not that I'd been short of unsuitable offers you understand, but single men in their fifties are thin on the ground and the surplus of attractive thirty and forty something women, in the nymphomania stage of life, tend to snap up those that are available. Women that age are like an explosion of a super nova star before it shrinks back to a white dwarf and I hear Viagra is the new male menopause drug of choice. I'd had my super nova with Fireman Sam ten years earlier, before falling into the black hole of The Last Chance Saloon. Time had been called and the towels were already being thrown over the pumps.

I think my mirror must have once belonged to Snow White's step mother, because it always spoke the truth. It was now telling me I was no longer a contender for the fairest in the land. Abandoned in my thirties, with two young children to bring up alone, life hadn't been easy and time had etched its passing onto my face. The loneliness, the isolation, had all taken their toll as I worked hard to forge a better life for myself and the kids. And then Fireman Sam, my saviour, arrived on the scene only to disappear after six years of all-consuming passion. He took a piece of my heart and never gave it back. But the days of self-pity were long since over; feeling sorry for yourself does nothing but drag you down even further. So, as I looked in the mirror, I thought about all the things that had happened in my life, the good, the bad and the really terrible, and I knew I didn't regret any of it. My face may be lined and my eyes may not sparkle as brightly as they used to, but the route my life had taken had made me strong, and I couldn't imagine wanting to be anyone else. I was confident that when the Grim Reaper made his call, I wouldn't be haunted by thoughts of 'what if', and 'if only'. I'd done the best I could with what life had offered me. I hadn't always made the right choices but I had never shrunk away from anything out of fear. Life is for living, not for existing in a safe haven, forever wondering what might have been.

Which brings me to Legion; not his real name but it's a fitting pseudonym. He was from Liverpool and for reasons of brevity I'm going to refer to him from here on as Leg. He was Master Class at getting one over on people, both mentally and physically, and I hadn't seen him in ten years. It's a bit of an understatement to say he was a tad unreliable all those years ago, but people change, not often, but sometimes they do. We met on an internet dating site a week or so after my relationship with Fireman Sam had ended. I was patched up with sticking plaster and looking for a replacement, and there was Fireman Leg; a Dubai delinquent in the making. I should have known better but, like most women, there's something about a fireman that's hard to resist. Maybe it's the brown baggy coveralls that make them look like teddies, or maybe it's the way they hold their hose pipes. Yes, yes, I know you've heard all the corny jokes before so I'll stop there. On a scale of one to ten, Leg was about a three, but he grew on me. He was single, which is rare for a fireman over thirty, and we had some good times together for a few months. All too soon he asked me to move in with him. I asked him if he was crazy, we hardly knew each other and I had my children to consider. Besides, the messages he was giving out were more mixed up than socks at a jumble sale. Things took a turn for the worse when he offered to take me and the kids to the cinema to see *Men in Black*. Six thirty came and went. Seven o'clock. The kids were getting fractious. Where he is? I tried to ring him. He didn't pick up. I left voicemail. He didn't ring back. Eventually I packed the kids into the car and off we went to spend the night munching on over-priced popcorn, swilled down with an unusual coloured iced drink that tasted like it contained battery acid. It wasn't the most enjoyable night I'd ever had; being stood up is almost as bad as being mugged.

In the morning my nine year old woke me to tell me Princess Diana had died. That was the last straw and I spent the whole day in tears. Leg contacted me a few days later and apologized with his usual charm and armed with a good excuse. His excuses were always amazingly convincing but if you cross-examined him he contradicted himself faster than a Ferrari lapping a Skoda. Sadly, I'm not a Barrister and I was an emotional mess so I forgave him. The following year I was offered a job a hundred miles away. Leg said he didn't want a distance relationship. Fine by me; I moved, lock stock and barrel with my boys, to a new life. Firemen were off the menu.

Fast forward three years and up he pops again; on the doorstep of my old home, asking the new owners for my contact details. They rang me, could they give him my telephone number? I was curious so I said okay.

He rang, "I can't live without you. I haven't been able to stop thinking about you. Will you marry me?"

It's a well known fact that, no matter how remote the chances of success, persistence can pay off. He was the dog and I was the cat he was chasing, (I was going to use the analogy of a cat and mouse, or a dog and a rabbit, but I absolutely refuse to denigrate myself in that way. A cat is fine, I have no objection to being a cat). When he had me firmly clenched in his teeth, he shook and he shook until I gave in. Come on girls, he said he was crazy about me. Tearful phone calls in the middle of the night, begging me to take him back. He said he'd do anything to make things right. Time was running out, would I get another chance like this? I lived in a rural back water of England where men were a scarce commodity and I hadn't seen hide nor hair of a single man for years. So I capitulate. After all, we get on well, and he's all the things I find attractive; manly, moody, his own person. Sadly the bliss lasted less than a week. My Guardian Angel appeared before me, disguised as the great and mighty Google. If it hadn't been for Larry Page and Sergey Brin it could have taken me months to discover he was already married. Why do people always blame 'the other woman' when nine times out of ten it's her that's the victim! So that was that. The end, (again). Bastard. Fortunately I was too busy with my new life to care. I was over him completely within a few minutes.

The soap opera, that is the life of a divorcee, has now rolled on another ten years and look, here he is again, popping up on Facebook like one of those ducks at the fairground. He's fifty years old now and says he's changed. So instead of shooting him down I wait and see what he has to say. He's more ugly than I remember, but that's being unfair. I don't suppose I'm the Farrah Fawcett clone that he remembers. Anyway, I don't bear grudges and I have a very short memory for knives that cause only superficial wounds. It's the deep cuts that leave scars.

"I'm in Dubai now. Love it. Got a really good job; Station Officer. Fantastic salary. I've never forgotten you. I'm single. You'd love it here, come and visit me. Just think, we could have been a couple for the last ten years."

"YOU WERE MARRIED!"

"Was I? We were always separating, split up years ago. Come on, we need to make up for lost time."

So, the unreliability, the contradictions, the mixed messages were all explained. His marriage had been on the rocks and he'd been looking for comfort elsewhere. The conversations and the flirting went on in cyberspace for the next three months. I stalled as long as I could but when he still sounded keen, and given my recapitulation in front of the mirror, I decided to accept his invitation. He said he'd have two weeks off work to show me round but there was one condition; he wasn't prepared to sleep on the settee in his one bed apartment, so if I went I'd either have to rough it in the lounge or sleep with him. Umm . . . I had been very attracted to him all those years ago. He was quite a bit younger than me and had a boyish charm that I found hard to resist. A romantic fling in Dubai was just what I needed. I thought of Arabian nights, bazaars and souks, and hot sweaty encounters on dhows in the harbor. So I put away the mirror and booked a flight without further ado.

'Bring it on,' I thought, as I prepared to fly off to my date with destiny.

KARA CLARKE

CHAPTER 2: The Reunion

The United Arab Emirates (UAE) consists of seven emirates, including Dubai, each with its own ruler. An emirate can be likened to a country or state within a larger confederate; in the way England, Scotland, Northern Ireland and Wales are all part of the United Kingdom; at least for the time being. There's a President (Chief of State) overseeing all the Emirates and also a Prime Minister who is head of the government. This was all news to me, I knew nothing about Dubai and hadn't had time to find out before jumping on a plane; this is what I read in the flight magazine that was tucked in the seat pocket in front of me. It seems there are no political parties, "the rulers hold power on the basis of their dynastic position and their legitimacy in a system of tribal consensus." A fancy way of saying this is only a democracy by virtue of the fact that the ruling elite decide who will rule.

It was almost midnight when the plane started its descent into Dubai airport. At three thousand feet, the city was a galaxy of different coloured lights surrounded on three sides by a deep, black void of desert where Arabian oryx and foxes roam. Dubai lies along the southern coast of the Persian Gulf, on the Arabian Peninsula, and I could see dhows idling on the water, their lights twinkling in the heat. The sight of them filled me with excitement and anticipation. I hoped, no expected, that I'd go back home with romantic memories of magical nights spent making up for lost time. The plane dropped lower and circled over the desert, an empty blackness. Amazing to think that all there was here not too long ago were nomadic cattle herders and pearl divers. Modern Dubai came about because of the discovery of oil in 1966 and all I knew about the city was what I'd seen on the emails circulated by well meaning friends; the amazing light show on the water, the Khalif tower, the highest building in the world, the rooftop pools with water cascading over the edge like a computer-generated Victoria Falls. I had butterflies in my stomach. So much that was new to me blended seamlessly into an anticipation of the future.

Once in the airport, I joined one of the nine queues waiting to go through Passport Control. The five foot nothing officer checking my queue, and wearing what looked like a table cloth, was like a bad case of constipation, whereas the other queues were moving faster than intestinal contents after a generous helping of prunes. My man was interrogating everyone to the nth degree. In between victims he was laughing and joking in Arabic with passing colleagues. I was pouring with sweat in the thirty five degree heat, unable to remove my leather jacket as I struggled, without success, to keep hold of my suitcase, my carry on case and four litres of spirits; four times that allowed into the UK. Given that it's a Muslim country and it's against the law to sell or consume alcohol in public places, this struck me as a bizarre contradiction! I learned later that non-Muslim residents are required by law to apply for a liquor licence if they wish to consume alcohol in their own home. As I struggled with my load, the litre bottle of Remy Martin I'd bought Leg as a gift, crashed onto the floor. I'm still having nightmares about what may have happened if it had broken.

I emerged from border control at 2am, two hours later than arranged, and I breathed a sigh of relief when I saw that Leg was there to greet me as promised. He looked much older than his photos and his head was reflecting the overhead lights with shining clarity. I don't remember seeing a photo of his hairlessness. Not a problem. Baldness can be very sexy. I think of Yul Brynner, in *The King and I*, and get a tingle down my spine. He told me later that he shaves his head to hide a receding hairline and has to massage his scalp with Vaseline everyday to stop it flaking. Ah well. When he greets me I sense a feeling of disappointment. Perhaps he was expecting Farrah. After a seven hour flight and queuing up in stifling heat for two hours, I probably don't look my best.

I think about the Aquagel packed safely inside my suitcase and hope it has survived the journey. I'm also hoping it's not a banned substance as I had heard that even over the counter medication can land you with a four month jail sentence here. I'd purchased the Aquagel the week before, and the young girl who served me wanted to know what it was used for as she'd never heard of it and didn't think they sold it.

"Yes of course you sell it," I'd whispered, "And please keep your voice down."

"So what's it for?" she asked again, in a horribly loud voice.

"Just go and ask the Pharmacist," I hissed, spitting venom across the counter.

The Aquagel finally appeared and she waved it around in a flamboyant gesture in front of the gathering audience, asking me did I want a bag.

"Yes, yes, I want a bag. Put it in a bag. NOW!"

Having secured my purchase, I'd slinked away with my embarrassment into the melee of shoppers and made my way to the perfume counter to treat myself to a bottle of 'Beautiful'. It held memories of a dirty weekend in Betws-y-Coed when Leg had said he'd never smelled anything so intoxicating. He'd been putty in my hands. So even if I didn't look too good at the moment, at least I knew I smelled irresistible.

We load my stuff into his Toyota and set off to his apartment. He tells me he's recently changed his job and is now working in Abu Dhabi where he has another apartment that he uses during the week. I ask him why he's changed his job when he loved the job he had in Dubai. Silently I wonder why he didn't tell me this before. He recites a long tale of how the company wasn't adhering to Health and Safety guidelines and how it was all going to blow up in their faces and he didn't want to be around when it did, or something like that. He tells me that his new job is with a company contracted to provide fire service cover for the Palace Guard, this being part of the UAE armed forces headquartered in Abu Dhabi and responsible for the defense of the seven emirates.

It all sounds very impressive and I want to know more. He says there's nothing more to tell, except that he's in the process of obtaining security clearance for the many different levels and different areas within the palace and the buildings under its jurisdiction. By way of changing the subject, Leg points to a thirty foot billboard we're just passing. It shows a man with a tea towel on his head, whose gleaming white teeth would have blinded me in full sunshine,

"That's Crown Prince Sheikh Hamdan bin Mohammed bin Rashid al Maktoum, also known as Fazza," Leg says, "He's 29; and next in line to rule Dubai."

He's very handsome. Leg pulls a Wikipedia print out from the fascia of the car and passes it to me. I learn from this that Fazza is his pen name; he likes to write poetry. His father has another twenty one children scattered around the emirates. Hopefully not all borne by Fazza's mother Sheikha Hind bint Maktoum bin Juma Al Maktoum. It seems

Fazza has a passion for camels, cars and skydiving, the vision that that conjures up in my mind is not a pretty sight; for him or the camel. It seems he's very rich and can afford to buy as many camels as he likes so I guess the demise of one sky diving camel is neither here nor there.

The next page tells me that Dubai has been ruled by the Al Maktoum dynasty since 1833. Its current ruler, Fazza's father, Sheikh Mohammed bin Rashid Al Maktoum, lives in the palace in Abu Dhabi as he is also the Prime Minister and Vice President of the UAE. Khalifa bin Zayed Al Nahyan is President of the UAE, Ruler of Abu Dhabi and Supreme Commander of the Armed Forces. I ask if he lives in the same palace as Fazza and his family. Leg says he can't talk about who lives where; it's not allowed. I don't think he knows, besides, all the Als, Sheikhs and Maktoums are probably making his head spin as much as mine. The print out tells me that the Al Nahayan's are a branch of the House of Al-Falahi, which is a branch of the Bani Yas tribe, and that they are related to the House of Al-Falasi from which the Al Maktoum's are descended. There's been a lot of in breeding then? Not that we English have any room to talk; pot calling the kettle springs to mind. Leg thinks Fazza is engaged to his cousin – Fazza's cousin, not Leg's. A brief footnote tells me that the presidential palace is situated in Ras Al Akhdar but that there are plans to build a new palace complex covering nearly two million square feet and, as well as the main palace, will have lots of smaller palaces for all the hangers on. That's one big palace. Leg tells me that the Emiratis are the elite ruling class; the untouchables. If an Emirati runs into the back of your car, it's your fault. If you can't pay what is commonly referred to as blood money, they put you in jail and throw away the key. At least that's what Leg said.

We talk about how great it is to see each other again. How it only seems like yesterday since we last met. We don't mention past misdemeanors. Half an hour later and we pull into a secure complex of flat roofed, multi-storey apartment blocks called, not very exotically, Motor City, so named because of its close proximity to the Dubai Autodrome racing circuit that tells visitors to "Fasten your seatbelts and get ready for the ride of your life". It sounds promising. A guard, dressed in black, sits in the brightly lit kiosk and nods sulkily in response to Leg's wave as he raises the barrier for us to enter. Leg acts like he's an old pal but it's obvious that the guard has little regard for him, we gained entry because of the resident's badge in the front window of his car.

A Pass Card allows us entry into the apartment building and a lift takes us up to the fourth floor. The apartment looks dreary in the dim, utility electric lights. The front door leads into one large room, which houses a kitchen at one end and a seating area with flat screen TV at the other. An old fashioned 1970s style teak dining table sits between them, next to an ironing board and a small computer desk. He's eager to show me the en suite bedroom that lies beyond the door by the TV. Not being in the mood to throw myself onto the kingsize bed, screaming "Take me, take me", the tour passes off without incident. Returning to the main area he announces he must leave as he has to be at work in a few hours.

"But I thought . . . "

"No, I haven't been able to book time off. The bastard in charge of the shift pattern hasn't worked it out yet. I'll be back on Wednesday though." Today was Sunday; well actually the early hours of Monday morning.

There's a map of Dubai sprawled out on the kitchen

counter. He shows me where we are. We appear to be midway across the sprawling metropolis that is Dubai. The main shopping area, given the Americanised label of Downtown Dubai, is almost 20 miles away. Dubai Mariner isn't much closer but is in the opposite direction. Both look a long way away for someone who doesn't have any transport. I ask him if he has any friends I can hang out with whilst he's at work. He says not. He tells me that his women friends are Emiratis and they won't have anything to do with European women. I learned later that he probably meant to say all his female friends are Chinese or Filipino, as he definitely didn't have any Emirati contacts at all.

"What about your male friends?"

"Oh no, they're all hairy arsed firemen, uncouth and rough. You don't want to be hanging out with them," Actually I wouldn't mind! Sounds like fun. But it's clearly not an option he's offering.

"What about your brother?" he'd already told me he lived in the next apartment block in the same complex, "Can you give me his telephone number?"

"I don't see why not, but I'll have to ask him first. I'll ring you tomorrow."

And then he went, but not before mentioning that he felt a little disappointed that I hadn't flung myself on the bed and shouted, 'Take me'.

KARA CLARKE

CHAPTER 3: The Dirty Truth

It's now 3am in the morning but my body thinks it's 11o'clock at night and I'm not tired. A cup of tea would be good. I find a few sachets of old coffee and tea bags in a dusty cupboard, all lifted from hotel rooms too long ago. I open the fridge. Beer. I count the cans. Twenty six. There's a mouldy piece of cheese in the door and a flat, freeze-burned piece of a dead animal in the freezer compartment. It looks suspiciously like a small rodent that's been trod on. There's no milk. I decide to pass on the tea and instead drink some of the duty free Jack Daniels whilst I unpack my case. I find a single pop sock in one of the bedside tables. I put it in the bin. I open the wardrobe; he has a lot more clothes than he used to have. Many designer labels. If I knew who they were I'd probably be impressed. There's not much space for my stuff but no worries, I travel light these days and don't take up much room; at least not in the wardrobe. After arranging my toiletries and cleansers, make-up and nail varnish, sun screens and body lotions in the en suite bathroom, (I don't travel THAT light!) I decide I should go to bed. That's when I see them. How come I hadn't noticed them before? Perhaps I was too embarrassed to look closely at the place where I might lose my virginity for the second time. Celibacy has that effect on you; it enshrouds you in your pre-sexual hang-ups. But there was no mistake. I hadn't seen semen stains like this since Fireman Sam's demise and they hit me in the gut like a well aimed punch. Unmistakable, white, misty stains streaked carelessly over the dark purple of the cover. I fling the duvet to one side. There are even more underneath. I feel sick. I feel like crying. He told me he was single and that he wasn't seeing anyone, so does this mean he's having one night stands with God knows what sort of women. I quickly strip the bed and fling all the linen in the washing machine on the hottest wash. I sit and watch it go round and round until I'm too tired to care. As I try to make myself comfortable on the settee, I wonder what sort of man invites a woman to stay in his apartment and leaves semen stains all over the bed. Or am I misjudging him; perhaps he's just been relieving himself in anticipation of my visit. I fall into a fitful sleep with this on my mind and dream about the geysers in Yellowstone, the next destination for my solo adventures.

When I wake a couple of hours later, I'm hungry. The squashed cheesy snack I'd saved from the plane will have to do for breakfast. I retrieve it from the bottom of my handbag and open it on the kitchen counter. There are small, dark coloured insects running around the sink area. They're skittish and hard to kill. On closer inspection I see they are newly hatched cockroaches; tiny replicas of their parents. Fortunately for me, though not for the cockroaches, I find a tub of white powder under the sink. The picture on the front shows a cockroach lying on its back with its legs in the air. I so hate killing anything but when terror strikes, needs must, so I sprinkle it all over the counter and under the sink before tucking into my squashed snack. After hanging out the washed bed linen on the blisteringly hot balcony, I venture outdoors to find some food and water. It may be November but the temperature is still hovering around thirty five degrees and despite the sultry, oppressive heat, I have my legs, shoulders and arms covered in deference to the country's religious rules. This means I'm very hot. I pass a swimming pool where an attendant is idling away the time, sweeping the already clean tiles. He looks bored and underpaid and pays me no attention. I turn another four corners and walk down another four streets that lead nowhere. I've no water and my thirst is beginning to rival Captain Anson's in *Ice Cold In Alex*. There's no one around, the place looks deserted and the heat haze is causing strange contortions of the environment, which is quite un-nerving. It takes me another half an hour to find my way out of the complex, which seems a fitting psychological metaphor for how I'm feeling. I walk past the guard in the kiosk and smile. He looks at me without any acknowledgement and carries on doing whatever it is he's doing. There's a cat sitting under a rose bush opposite his kiosk, stretching its sinewy body like a ballerina learning the grand plie. I whisper a greeting and he meows back, emphasizing the coldness of the guard's dismissal of me. I adore cats. We have an affinity that's hard to explain on a pragmatic level. The feline fraternity are part of my soul family; my power animals.

It's a good half a mile to the shops; mainly coffee houses and takeaways. I smile amiably at everyone I pass. If they look friendly, I even proffer a cheery good morning. By the time I get to the supermarket, another five hundred yards along the hot pavement, I've given up and have become as unsociable and un-communicative as everyone else. It doesn't seem like a very friendly place to be hanging out on your own. I throw a handful of things into my basket; a piece of fish and some salad. Milk, butter, bread rolls and jam. I include half a dozen eggs and a large bottle of water. How much did she say? 200 dirhams! That's about £40 in sensible money. No wonder everyone looks miserable! I check the till receipt as I make my way back to the apartment. Eggs 30 dirhams!! That's almost £1 each! Don't they have chickens in Dubai? By the time I get back it's three o'clock and too late to think about trying to get into the city. I clean the apartment instead, paying particular attention to the bathroom and the kitchen. I notice a door in the entrance lobby. Thinking it will be a broom cupboard, I open it hoping to find a vacuum cleaner. I find a cloakroom containing a toilet and a sink. To the left of the sink, and hanging from a towel rail, in all their glory, are several pairs of recently washed scanty women's panties, hung there to dry. This is too much! I take a photograph of them to send to my friends back home. They'll never believe this. There's a calendar hanging on the wall by the TV. There are no entries so I make one by circling the 20th November and writing underneath,

"Oh I forgot! Kara coming to stay for 2 weeks. Damn - forgot to move the panties from the bathroom."

I'm well aware that whatever he's been up to during my ten year absence is absolutely nothing to do with me, so I don't mention any of this to him when he texts me later in the day to say he'll come over after work tomorrow and stay the night. The jury's out about how I feel about that but at least I won't be stuck here alone. When it goes dark at five thirty, I bring in the bedding from where it's been drying on the balcony. On shaking the duvet cover, a cockroach at least six inches long (okay I'm exaggerating!) drops out onto the tiled floor and scurries away at the speed of light, somewhere where I can't find it. I hunt round, move the bed, move the bedside cabinets. There are no holes, cracks or crevices that it could be hiding in, but I can't find any trace of it. I tell myself it's just one of God's creatures and it's not its fault it's in the bedroom. And it's not its fault it's a cockroach either, it doesn't mean me any harm, it's just a cockroach doing what cockroaches do; someone's got to come back as a cockroach, we can't all be human. What's the worst it can do to me?

Crawl over me in the middle of the night, that's what! Or worse still, decide to take up residence in the warm, wet cavern that is my mouth! I banish that thought and go and cook my tea in the cockroach infested kitchen and eat it in front of the TV on the settee that will probably be my bed for the next fortnight. I have my bottle of Jack Daniels for company and we settle down to watch four films back to back, Avatar, Double Jeopardy and two others I've already seen, so memorable I can't even remember what they were.

KARA CLARKE

CHAPTER 4: Some Really Bad News

It's 8am. Three men enter the apartment. Two of them are wearing dark suits and seem to be in the employment of the third man. They come into the bedroom and threaten to hurt me if I don't comply. The third man removes all his clothes and steps onto the bed above me. He's standing astride me and I can see his genitals with glorious lucidity! I ask him what the hell he thinks he's doing but nothing comes out of my mouth. He lowers himself on top of me . I try to scream. Silence. I think I'm awake but it turns out I'm not. It's one of those weird experiences we all have from time to time, where we're still dreaming but are convinced we've woken up. They're called false awakenings. Not sure how I felt about having had this one.

I get up and dress hurriedly. I feel ill at ease. The apartment suddenly feels like a whore house. I text Leg, wanting to know what time he'll be here. He doesn't reply. I go to the supermarket again and buy enough food for dinner for two. He texts at 2pm with no mention of coming over. Instead he asks me what I'm up to and suggests I go into Dubai and take the brown bus tour.

"How do I get into Dubai?"

"Taxi. They're cheap as chips."

When I ask if he's still coming over he claims to have no recollection of saying he would, and if he did, he meant tomorrow. I walk back to the supermarket looking for a taxi rank. No sign. I ask an American where I should go to find one. She tells me you can't hail taxis, it's illegal, you must ring and order one. She gives me a telephone number and tells me I must press 2 as soon as someone answers, otherwise it will go through to an operator speaking in Arabic. It's now 3pm, only two hours of daylight left. I decide it wouldn't be wise to be a woman alone in Dubai at night so I go back to the apartment. This visit is quickly turning into a holiday from hell. I've been here two days and seen nothing but the inside of a supermarket and an ex-lover's cockroach infested apartment. I've travelled on my own many times, America, Europe, New Zealand, but I've never felt this alone before. I feel like I've been abandoned in a country with a culture I don't understand and know too little about. It doesn't feel good.

I sign in to Skype, hoping for someone to talk to. A friend in the Netherlands is online and we chat about his life for a while. And then a friend in England signs in. I bring her up to date. She suggests I Google Motor City to try and find out if there are any social events planned in the area. She's a good friend to have; always so sensible. And then my friend in Estonia rings. I tell her about my lucid dream of this morning. She understands that some dreams can contain information not available to our waking mind, even the possibility of a psychic intrusion, and she understands why it made me anxious. She suggests I buy candles to bring light into the apartment; a way of cleansing bad energy. After signing off I find a dedicated Motor City website. I register and leave a message on the board asking if there is anyone alive in Motor City. No one responds so I guess there isn't. I make my third trip to the supermarket that day and emerge with an armful of tea lights and lavender scented pillar candles. It's already dark but I'm craving some human contact and so I call in Starbucks for a coffee. I feel uncomfortable on my own; it isn't like me to feel this way. Two men sit at the table by the door with their laptops open, discussing business. Three women heavily made up and with shoes that could skewer a person through, are whispering in the corner. An important looking man, dressed in the traditional attire, is waving his finger at his three companions; they look like puppies who've had their noses smacked. The young girl behind the counter checks her watch; she wants to go home. A young man stands at her side with a peevish, sullen look on his face. Usually I don't give my aloneness a second thought but I'm getting suspicious looks that are making me feel conspicuous and causing a deep moat to form around my little table; a barrier of isolation. I go back to the apartment and light six of the candles. After a dinner of fresh fish and rice salad I settle down to another evening watching TV.

Around ten o'clock I see something move out of the corner of my eye in the area that leads to the front door. I tell myself it's just my imagination working overtime because of the bad dream. Then again, it could be the six inch cockroach. Whatever it was, it spooked me and made me feel uneasy. I didn't dare close my eyes after that so I stayed up until I was so tired that I wouldn't have noticed if a six foot cockroach had walked past. Unable to muster up any enthusiasm for sleeping on the couch, I crawled into the king size bed in the early hours of the morning.

I tossed and turned for a long time; unable to sleep. At 3.30am my mobile phone makes a noise like a sparrow being trod on. I reach out and fumble round for it in the dark. It's a text from my neighbour back home. I know this isn't going to be good news. Her husband, a dear friend of mine, was diagnosed with prostate cancer last year. The prognosis wasn't good and he'd been taken ill a few days before I left for Dubai. The consultant, however, advised that he probably still had many months left. The text said that he'd died two hours ago. I'm devastated. I get up and try to deal with it. I tell myself to stay calm, take deep breaths, don't give in to the panic that I feel rising in my gut. It's no good. The tears start and won't stop. I want someone to talk to; a hug would be good. I sign on to Skype but everyone's asleep. Memories of this same week in November, twenty one years ago, come flooding back. The sort of memories that leave traces like old tea stains on best china. An 18-30 reunion weekend and a message from my sister that my brother has been found dead in his caravan. Suicide. He was 48. The friends I were with at the time were at the stage of life where drinking and partying took precedence over offering sympathy and support, so I'd done my grieving alone. Twenty four hours in a Butlins' chalet with only a bag of crisps and a can of coke for company is the worst sort of initiation into grief that I know. Remembering all this doesn't help.

I go back to bed at 7am and try to sleep. It's useless. I get up and go to the pool. I text Leg. He says he'll come over this afternoon after work and give me a big hug. With the sun on my face and a good book to read, I start to feel a little better. I so desperately need some company and I'm looking forward to Leg arriving more than I can say. He said he'll be here at 4pm; only another few hours. The way I feel, I'm prepared to forgive him anything. I go back to the apartment just before four to shower and change. My eyes are still swollen and puffy but it's surprising what a bit of eye shadow and mascara can disguise. I think about decanting some Aquagel into a small pot, ready for discrete application. I remember the overwhelming urge to have someone love me when my brother died; a way to prove that even though a part of me had died, the bigger part of me was still alive. I decide not to tempt fate. I put on a pretty dress and fix my hair, pour myself a Jack Daniels and wait. At 5.30pm I text him to ask if I should be worried that he hasn't arrived. I give him fifteen minutes but he doesn't reply. I text him again. Still no response. I'm worried. What if something's happened to him? At 6.30pm I sign on to Facebook and try to contact his brother who lives in an apartment in the next block and whose phone number he'd promised to give me. His brother has no email link and so I post on his wall,

"I'm really worried about Leg. He was supposed to be here at 4pm and hasn't turned up. He knows that a friend of mine has just died and I'm in bits."

A voice speaks inside my head, I don't know if it's my Higher Self, my Intuition, my Guardian Angel or the first sign of schizophrenia; it says,

"He's let you down so many times before and he's just done it again!"

His brother responds immediately,

"I've just spoken to him on the phone and he's fine. Where are you? He's never mentioned you. I can't believe he's just left you sitting in his apartment without telling anyone."

The tears are rolling down my cheeks again. How could he do this to me?

"What's going on?" I post again on his brother's wall, "Is he married?"

At eight twenty my phone rings. He's mad at me for contacting his brother and denies vehemently that he's married.

"There's women's pants in the bathroom, and semen stains on the bedding, and you keep saying you're coming round and then you don't."

"When I said I'd come over, I was thinking it was Thursday, not Wednesday. I got the days mixed up." That's the most lame excuse he's ever come up with.

"And yes, I entertain a lady now and again okay! I'm not a monk. I'll see you tomorrow without fail." Call terminated.

My friend in Estonia rings through on Skype. She tells me it's not my fault, that any woman my age would have taken a chance on a man who said he still wanted her. Her advice, delivered in her delightful pidgin English, is straight to the point,

"When he arrive tomorrow, slap his face and kick him in goolies." Well, that's what I want to do but I have to take some of the blame for this. I was stupid to think he could have changed. Stupid for trying to turn back the clock, and stupid for dwelling on old memories. But it's time for honesty on both sides. I'm not here simply to rekindle an old flame. If he was living back in England I doubt I'd have even returned his messages. I like to travel but I don't like package holidays. What more can I say?

I take off the pretty dress and put on jeans and T-shirt, slamming the wardrobe door so hard that the whole room shudders. I feel better. And then my English friend rings; the sensible one. She talks the light of reason, advising me to be really nice to him when he finally puts in an appearance. I'm to tell him how upset I am about my friend's death and how disappointed I was that he didn't turn up when he said he would, but that I'm very glad to see him now and am looking forward to a wonderful weekend of sightseeing with him. Like she said, the alternative is to pack my case and sleep on the street.

She sends me a link to a website that has a list of expat events in Dubai. There are numerous coffee mornings listed where new people are always welcome. Maybe I can go along and hopefully find some new friends to hang out with. Half a bottle of Jack Daniel's later, I go to bed, perchance to sleep. It's just turned midnight and I take an over the counter sleep aid. I'm woken at 2.45am by another text from my neighbour, telling me the date of the funeral. She's not widely travelled and the time difference doesn't occur to her. An hour later and I'm up again with painful IBS symptoms. I take a double dose of prescribed medication and a couple of painkillers and try to go back to sleep.

KARA CLARKE

CHAPTER 5: A Night Out

It's Thursday. This is my fourth day in the United Arab Emirates. I've endured four sleepless nights and the death of a friend and am not feeling too good. However, the weekend starts at 4pm today and Leg has promised to spend two days showing me the Dubai sights. I've had a whole lifetime of practice in bundling up sadness in bubble wrap and putting it away in a dark cupboard, so that's what I do and hope for the best. I go down to the pool in the morning. I read. I swim. There's no one there except me and the pool attendant, who still looks disinterested and underpaid.

Leg arrives unexpectedly at 2pm. I've no make-up on and my eyes are still puffy but he doesn't seem to notice. His light hearted banter and ready smile help dispel my grey mood and apprehension. Yes, I'm a push over. But I hate confrontation and really, what choice do I have? I have a long, fun-filled, sight-seeing weekend to look forward to, starting with a meal tonight in Dubai, hopefully with a good view of the light show. I shower and change and, for the second time that week, don my prettiest dress, before heading off to the city. It's a long drive and the traffic is horrendous and at a standstill in places. There's something about sitting in traffic jams that affects people badly; it's not good for relationships. You've only to take a peek inside cars stuck on the M6 on a Bank Holiday Monday to understand what I mean. It opens a void inside the human brain that causes all sorts of memories to jump in and fill the space, uninvited and unannounced, good and bad. Sadly, given my experiences of the last few days, it was mainly the bad ones that made the leap, and when he started talking about how wonderful our relationship was all those years ago, they acted like they'd been given a shot of growth hormone. He tells me about the time he needed to think things over and so flew off to Benidorm with his mates. He says he remembers it well because it was the weekend that Princess Diana died. I want to do to him what my Estonian friend suggested but he's driving and I'm trying to hang on to my fun-filled, sight-seeing weekend. The memory of me and the kids watching *Men in Black* alone flashes into my mind with more clarity than a Hollywood movie in full technicolour. The Sword Maiden in me picks up all the virtual weapons I can conjure up and I launch them, one by one, at the lying, cheating, excuse for a man sitting beside me. When I've finished reminding him of his past transgressions, I start on the panties in the bathroom and the semen stains on the bed. Leg's truth is very elusive and tends to change from day to day, so this time I'm treated to another version of it. The Chinese girlfriend whom he loved and lost two years ago, did not go back to China like he told me, she went to Abu Dhabi and they live there together Sunday to Thursday. The panties are hers; they like to spend the weekend in Dubai.

"She doesn't mind me having sex with other women," he says, "providing I wear a condom, only have sex with them once and always go back to her."

!!!!!! PLEEEEASE!!!!!!!!

The next thing I know I'm fighting for the rights of a woman I've never even met.

"So what are you saying? That she's so frightened of losing you that she'll let you do as you please?"

I tell him that to take advantage of a woman like that is, frankly, appalling. Has he no morals? Does he think so little of her, to treat her in such a cavalier way? Poor woman, my heart goes out to her. He talks back at me with his excuses and justifications. Has he really just said that this is how all relationships are in the UAE? He jostles his words with more skill than a ferret wriggling out of a mouse hole. By the time we get into the city, we're in the middle of World War III. We have to call a truce. There's a twinkle in his eye when he reminds me about the risqué rendezvous we had on top of Great Orme back in the glory days. I remember it well, it should have been a week on a Greek island to make the most of my ex-husband's all-too-rare offer to have the kids for a week. He stalled over the Greek promise and then downgraded it to a week in Blackpool. I turned that offer down, there's something very tacky about a kiss-me-quick hat and a grope under the North Pier. Then came the news that he had urgent Territorial Army manoeuvers that he couldn't get out of; that's the reason I ended up with nothing more than a weekend in Betws-y-Coed, which, to be fair, included an exciting excursion into Llandudno. My diary at the time recorded the irony of rolling round on Great Orme with him when probably Little Orme would have been more appropriate.

With my head full of these annoying memories, we finally pull into the car park at the great Dubai shopping mall. It's a huge complex on many floors and we window shop as he tries to remember where the restaurant is. Each floor has a central hub with wide avenues leading away in the four cardinal directions. The last time I saw so many designer outlets was on the Champs-Elysees, but even that can't compare to this. The prices in the windows of Carolina Herrera, Liu Jo, Stella McCartney, Gerard Darel, and such like, warn off those who can't afford 10,000 dirhams for a skirt or a handbag or a pair of Jimmy Choo shoes. He expects me to be impressed. I'm not. I tell him I don't even like shopping. He's shocked. In his world, it's the only thing women live for.

We make our way up to the top level. I'm expecting an expensive meal in a first class restaurant. He takes me to TGI Fridays and we have to queue for a table on the balcony. Still, it was worth waiting for. We're shown to a table that overlooks the Burj Khalifa Lake and are treated to a spectacular view of the famous light show, created by the same people who produced the Fountains of Bellagio in Las Vegas. This, however, is bigger and better. Of course it has to be, it's Dubai. We watch as twenty two thousand illuminated gallons of water are sprayed nearly five hundred feet into the air, and made to dance in sync to the music. Dubai is full of contradictions, and this is one of them. It's okay for water to dance but people are only allowed to dance at licensed clubs or in the privacy of their own home. Dancing in public is classed as indecent and provocative and will be punished. The waitress tells us that, tonight, the fountains are dancing to the Arab world's top-selling dance number Shik Shak Shok. I thought she said Shit Shag Shock and I laugh. She doesn't. Leg tells me it's an offence to use foul language, it's considered an obscene act punishable by jail or deportation. I go to the Ladies toilet and wash my mouth out with soap and water whilst praying for forgiveness. I think about my good friend and neighbour and his life cut short. It makes me more determined than ever to enjoy my time here, despite the company I'm keeping. Returning to the table, I order steak and a cocktail of lime juice and soda. Leg orders the same. Although Dubai is liberal when it comes to visitors bringing alcohol into the country, the government doesn't allow alcohol to be bought or consumed in public places. When the cocktails arrive, I marvel at their greenness, the like of which

I have never seen before. They are glowing with a strange inner light. I'm a bit concerned but Leg says it's nothing to worry about. Over dinner I learn that he hasn't told his Chinese girlfriend that I'm here. He tells me she'll be furious if she finds out and could turn nasty.

"Against whom?" I ask.

"She won't tolerate ex- girlfriends."

"Why? How many of them have been here?"

He shrugs.

I look at him over the rim of my green cocktail, which now has more fluorescence than genetically modified E.coli.

"No," I say.

"No what?" says he.

"No sex,"

He throws me a brief glance but says nothing. I tell him that he's forfeited that privilege as he's doing to me exactly what he did before. He's not as attentive after that. The waitress brings the bill. He doesn't look at it. I pick it up and offer to pay my share. I have the impression he's hoping I'll pay his share as well. Not on your TGI matey! On the way out we pass people queuing for the table we've just vacated. Our next stop is the bar at Dubai Beach. This is the place to see and be seen, a private haunt for ex-pats and those with more money than sense, and one of the few places where you can drink alcohol and dance. He buys me some cheap UK lager at the extortionate price of 46 dirhams, or £8 a pint. He says he's trying to make up for his transgressions. It tastes like cleaning fluid. Hundreds of leggy beauties parade up and down the walkway in front of us, long glossy hair flicked this way and that. Skirts only nearly worn, or hot pants with less fabric than a napkin; teetering through the soft sand on heels that add a foot to their height. They look ridiculous. I guess

I'm getting old. I see him drooling at them all, his eyes hungrily devouring the bare flesh. He tells me about a friend who's been called back to the UK, something about his visa having run out. He's asked Leg to look after his eighteen year old daughter whilst he's away. My God! If I had an eighteen year old daughter, Leg would be the last person I'd want to look after her! His attention is now diverted to his mobile phone as he tries to ring her. He rings several times and leaves several voice mails. When there's no response he resorts to sending her texts. I buy the next round and, on my return from the bar, he says she's texted back and has agreed to meet up with us. We wait at the appointed place for two hours. She doesn't show. We drive back to his apartment and sit and talk until 3am. He refuses to sleep on the couch, and so do I. We agree to sleep on each edge of the king size bed with an invisible barrier between us. After a few minutes, his hot little hand creeps over to my side, I smack it away.

CHAPTER 6: The Karma Kafe

It's Friday, the first day of the Islamic weekend and my first full day of sightseeing. I'm up at 7am with awful griping pains in my stomach. I make myself a cup of peppermint and fennel tea and sit on the toilet in the guest bathroom contemplating the panties, until all the contents of my digestive tract have been explosively expelled. I creep back to bed around 8am and pretend to be asleep. At nine o'clock he slides out of bed and into the en suite. Following a hissing sound, something highly scented seeps under the door and makes me sneeze. The door opens and he pounces on me in a parody of love making.

"I have to go out," he says, "pick a car up for my brother."

I say, "We were supposed to be going sightseeing!"

He says he'll be back at twelve. Great. Another morning marooned in his apartment. I get up and send my friends an email update. I can't decide whether my reports are received like a soap opera or a farce. Twelve o'clock comes and goes. There's only one key to the apartment & I've got it, and if he's not back in five minutes I'm going out to the shops to get some lunch.

He wasn't and I did. He finally turned up at 1.30pm saying he'd had to stop en route to Oman to discharge the contents of his intestines; bright green and smelling like a swamp. Yep, that sounds like the same stuff that poisoned me. Perhaps the waitress in TGI Fridays was an ex-girlfriend. I then get a garbled tale about how his brother, who owns two cars, a Dodge truck and a Trailblazer, had taken the Dodge truck to Oman yesterday, a one and a half hour drive away, to visit his girlfriend. When he got there, the girlfriend said she wanted to go out in the Trailblazer. So Leg had driven the Trailblazer up there, swapped it for the Dodge and driven back. The name of the truck apart, there sounded something very dodgy about it all. Clearly my sightseeing is no one's priority except mine.

"So what have you got planned for me today?"

"Well actually there's an Aussie interested in buying my Discovery. I need to strike whilst the iron's hot," yes, it seems he owns two cars as well,

"I've told him I'll meet him downtown at three."

"But you said . . ."

"Sorry, can't be helped. I can't pass up a buyer. You can come with me if you want."

"Why, thank you!"

So my sightseeing tour has morphed into another few hours sat in traffic jams, and the fireman has morphed into a second hand car salesman.

Soon we're ambling along the E44 highway in his Landrover Discovery, which moves like an old man running with two sticks of different lengths; all bumps and scrapes. Leg said it just needed the wheels balancing. He explained that the engine blew up on him last month and it had cost him fifteen thousand dirhams to have it replaced; almost as much as he'd paid for the car two months earlier. He said he didn't have the wheels balanced because he wanted to keep the costs down.

"Who, in their right mind, will buy a car that drives like this?"

"An Aussie."

He got the instructions for meeting the Australian wrong and we drove round and round Dubai in grid-locked traffic for over an hour. Finally we met up with him outside

Starbucks down by the Mariner. I have to give him his due, his sales talk was good.

"I want to be straight with you," he said to the guy, "I bought the car in September and the engine seized the week after. I had a new one put in and have spent a fortune getting it right. So it's in tip top condition now. Reliable? Oh God yes. Apart from the engine blowing up, it's never let me down."

He didn't tell him about the knocking and the juddering. The Aussie, wise man that he was, insisted on taking it for a spin.

"Ah that mate? That's nothing. I had new tyres put on and the wheels just need balancing, that's all. No worries."

The guy walked away and I breathed a sigh of relief; I'd started to feel like an accomplice.

Business unsatisfactorily terminated, he suggests that he take me up the iconic Khalifa Tower, which is accessed from the shopping mall. It takes almost an hour to drive back to downtown Dubai and into the car park, and another half hour walking through the Mall to the ticket office. When we finally get there we're told that all the tickets for the day have been sold. We wander round the mall again, window shopping again, though I'm more interested in people watching. The UAE natives are very easy to identify. The men wear the traditional kandura, sometimes known as thawbs, Leg calls them dishdash. On their heads they wear the guthra, tied with an egal, or in English speak, a tea towel held on with a bit of rope. The women cover their heads with a Shela, a loose fitting scarf that Leg points out will have a designer label; probably Dior or Givenchy. Most don't cover their faces and are strikingly beautiful in their elegant black Abaya robes. Though here is another contradiction. Leg says the traditional attire is worn only in public as a badge of honour, and that underneath their Abayas, they will be wearing sexy little western numbers. I'm guessing that's another one of his fantasies. Leg tells me that the Emiratis are the ruling class and act like royalty, regardless of their background. The Government encourages this, he says, by demanding that they are placed in key positions in all businesses based in the UAE. Leg said they are just figure heads; they don't do any work but take the praise for the success of the business or company. Each year His Highness Shaikh Mohammed bin Rashid Al Maktoum, honours the winners of the Dubai Government Excellence Programme (DGEP). This includes prestigious awards to Emiratis for almost everything, including distinguished new employee, distinguished female employee, distinguished employee in specialised job, distinguished technical and engineering employee, distinguished administrative and financial employee, distinguished government employee, distinguished team performance; you get the idea. No achievement, no matter how small, is left unrewarded. Leg tells me that all young Emiratis are given grants to study at foreign universities. The grant includes the price of three business class trips home every year. A blessed people indeed. Leg says he's always been on good terms with the Emiratis he's worked for because he knows how to manipulate them and play the system. They'd probably cut off his head if they heard him talking like that.

A short while later, we find ourselves at the aquarium, the centrepiece of the mall. An information board tells me it's one of the largest tanks in the world and has the world's largest viewing panel, a hundred feet wide and about thirty feet high. It contains more than thirty three thousand living animals, from eighty five different species, including over four hundred sharks and rays. A special 'lunar-cyclic' lighting system changes the ambience of the tank depending on the time of day so that the natural rhythm of the inmates isn't disrupted. As we watch the eels and the rays idling their life away, Leg tells me all about the joys of scuba diving. He's in the process of taking his Diving Master exams. I say I'd love to go scuba diving. He says I can't until I've undergone six weeks of training. He obviously doesn't want to take me. I wonder if he would if I slept with him.

"So how come tourists can scuba dive in every other country with only a few hours training?"

"They can't."

"Yes they can."

This is turning into another argument so I suggest we pay to walk through the tunnel that runs through the centre of the tank. Leg says the opportunity for a close encounter with some of the most fascinating underwater animals on the planet, is not worth the entrance fee. He wanders over to the exit tunnel and just walks right on in there, bold as you like. A security guard starts shouting. Leg takes no notice; perhaps he doesn't hear. I wonder if he's even aware of what he's doing. The guard runs into the tunnel and grabs Leg by the arm,

"You have to pay to come in here. Go to the ticket office and pay."

Leg doesn't want to pay and shows no sign of embarrassment or regret at having created such a spectacle. We wander off.

From our prime viewing spot in TGI Friday's the night before, I'd seen a bridge spanning the water and leading to what appeared to be an old part of the city, or should I say a modern part in the style of traditional Arabic architecture.

Leg tells me he's never been there and has no idea what it is, so I suggest we cross the bridge and find out. It turns out to be an indoor souk; a sort of bazaar, full of wonderful shops selling authentic crafts. Leg is bored. The only shops he's interested in are those that sell scuba diving gear. I buy a charcoal burner and some resin incense. I also buy a small paper map of the city, which would have been cheaper had it been made of gold leaf.

As we're idling along on the first floor, we stumble on The Karma Kafe; it looks inviting with its gold paintwork and ripe red, tiffany-style lamps in the windows. I try to peer inside but the light from the lamps doesn't penetrate that far, making the restaurant seem even more mysterious and inviting. In contrast, there's a soft orange glow spilling out of the open doorway and we wander inside to take a closer look. We find ourselves in a small reception hallway, dimly lit with Arabic pendant lamps, the source of the welcoming orange light. Today's menu has been carefully displayed on a free standing gold plinth, positioned to one side of a black glass door that hides the inner sanctum from sight. There are only four main dishes, a sign of a Master Chef restaurant, and they are very expensive. I'm so hungry I could eat a scabby dog but Leg says he's not and doesn't want to go in. I suggest he take a good look at The Karma Kafe because he'll be back here one day and may find he has to pay a higher price than what's shown here. He misses the point entirely and bustles me out hurriedly as a waiter is about to greet us. He decides we'll catch the light show again, this time right outside The Dubai Mall on the Lower Ground Waterfront Promenade. I promise myself I'll come back to the souk next week to buy presents for all my lovely friends back home.

There aren't many people milling around at the side

of the lake and we secure a good viewing point right at the front by the railings. Leg says the show repeats every fifteen minutes but there he is, wrong again. Nearly an hour later, the show starts and we find ourselves at the front of a sixteen deep crowd. The melodious voice of Sarah Brightman fills the air, accompanied by the majestic notes of the world-renowned Italian tenor, Andrea Bocelli, singing *Con te partiro*. Like the synchronistic Karma Kafe, I should have realized that our *Time to say goodbye* had already been and gone; and that this extension was good for neither man nor beast. There's a Japanese lady on my left, dressed in a bright yellow jacket, and holding a camera that would have impressed David Attenborough. Fortunately I see it coming from the corner of my eye and duck as she swings it round to get a panoramic view of the show. I take a few minutes of video with my little digital camera as the water jets dance and sway like demented water sylphs.

We get back to the car at around 7.30pm, still not having eaten, and spend the next two hours driving back to Motor City in heavy traffic. Stop. Start. Stop. Start. Whilst waiting at traffic lights, I comment on a group of labourers who are digging a new road, working through the night. Ten sandwich bags are lined up in a neat row in the dirt, each knotted carefully at the top. My heart goes out to the workers, they can't be any older than my own sons. Leg says it's cheaper to hire twenty men from India or Asia than it is to hire an excavator. He tells me that after paying for their lodgings, they'll be lucky to come out with a hundred dirhams a month. That's about £20. I'm appalled. This is the next thing to slavery. My concern for them annoys Leg and he launches into the most upsetting tirade of racial abuse I have ever heard. I can't listen to it and tell him to shut up. I'm shocked. So shocked, I feel sick. He says everyone in Dubai is of the same opinion. I don't believe him. I can't believe him. I remember a visit to Dachau and being filled with the same sense of dread when I stood in the Church of Atonement. It's horrific to realise that there's an aspect of humanity that is so destructive and bigoted that it cares nothing for other people. It has no empathy and no charity, no kindness and no love. And the scariest part of all is that we are all human and so are all capable of atrocities; it's part of human nature. It means we must all take responsibility for the horrors that are perpetrated in our world, and also take responsibility for the views expressed by other humans, no matter how perverse and unjust those views may be. We're all capable of discrimination, maybe it doesn't show itself as racism or sadism, it can just as easily be expressed against those we sit in judgment of; we're all tribal at heart. Yet it frightens me to think that people like Leg will never allow themselves to be enlightened, informed or educated because their world suits them just fine as it is. Providing they're not the ones at the bottom of the pile, they're all right Jack. I wonder what sort of a world we are rushing towards when our modern cities are nurturing such egocentric intolerance. Leg goes on to tell me, with pride in his voice, how he "got one over" on a taxi driver. Most of the taxi drivers are male and from Asia and they are subject to stringent regulations. The DTC Taxi Drivers Fines and Penalty Lists, details 101 offences, not only governing their behaviour whilst driving a taxi, but also whilst in their living accommodation. Given their wages, the fines for any transgression are more than they can pay, and it only takes a phone call from a passenger with a grievance to set the wheels of injustice in motion. These are not free men. Leg explains that they are contravening the regulations if they release the handbrake before switching on the meter. I discovered later that he was misinformed about this, the car must have travelled at least 2km with the meter switched off before it's deemed an offence. However, Leg used the threat of reporting the driver for just such a reason in order to get out of paying his fare. He demanded the driver take him on a long, circuitous route to his destination. On arrival, joyous and victorious, he refused to pay the fare. The driver could do nothing about it knowing that it would only take one phone call to get him sacked or thrown into prison, unable to pay the hefty fine. Leg celebrated with a good slap up meal and the best wine in the house. I tell him that what he did was immoral and I can't understand how he could behave that way without any remorse. He says he's going to start calling me his conscience. I hope he remembers this conversation when he finds himself back at The Karma Kafe.

We arrive back at Motor City around nine thirty pm, having stopped en route to buy a takeaway. Leg is eager to show me a video he's made of himself, that maps his career as a firefighter. Liverpool, Kuwait, Tehran, Oman, Dubai and finally Abu Dhabi. He's clearly very proud of himself; narcissist and egotist are words that spring to mind. When I first met him he was a retained fireman working as a techie in a national call centre. The first man at the station, when a shout comes in, gets to drive the Fire Engine so he bought a house just a few hundred yards away. At his own expense, he trained to be an airport fireman. None of this interesting detail is in his video. It seems he then got a job as an instructor at a well known UK Fire Service College. How he managed to get that I'll never know, he never was the sharpest knife in the drawer. I learned later that he was actually a sub-contractor, employed by his brother who goes by the grand title of Fire Service Consultant. I also learned later that Revenue and Customs are chasing them both for thousands of pounds in unpaid taxes accrued whilst doing contract work in Kuwait.

We chat about how wonderful he is until 2am and then go to bed; again me on one edge and he on the other. He tells me he's got a great day planned for me tomorrow, to make up for today. We're going quad biking in the desert and will stay until darkness falls so I can marvel at the stars set against the blackest sky I'll have ever seen. It sounds wonderful. I'll take my binoculars and pretend I'm with Brian Cox, that will add a bit more starlight.

CHAPTER 7: The Orgasm

This is a very short chapter. That's because this part of my story didn't last very long. I didn't sleep. I felt agitated inside as if every nerve in my body was on alert, though my physical body was so tired and heavy it just lay in the same position the whole night without moving. At 7am I became aware of an incredibly powerful surge of sexual energy around the root chakra, that's the area at the base of the spine, radiating out towards the genitals. I could feel the energy swirling and spiraling, and gaining in amplitude with every second that passed. It felt like it was coming from him. I tried to block it but it was too powerful. Never having dipped my toe into the waters of Tantra, I'm assuming this is what's known as Tantric energy. After a few minutes, I feel him move closer, almost imperceptibly like a thief in the night, hidden under the dark covers. Then his hand slides round my waist like a cobra. I try to move it but he holds on. It creeps up to my breasts, brushing the nipples with a gentle caress and then squeezing and pinching. It feels good, it's been such a long time. I know I should stop him but my hesitation is the cue he's been waiting for. The next thing I know, he's roughly pulled me over onto my back and is administering cunnilingus; biting and sucking. My body explodes in orgasm, and then another in quick succession, the result of energy surging up the chakras. I want to scream but I don't want to encourage him, so I don't make a sound. Now he's hurting me and I ask him to stop. He doesn't. I ask him again, this time more assertively. He still doesn't stop. I reach down to push him away. He gets the message. He gets up and goes to the bathroom. I can feel his anger pulsating in the air. I lie there immobile, hardly daring to breathe. Is this what my false awakening had been warning of? After a short while he walks into the lounge and I hear him pick up his keys. He's going to go out and leave me alone again without a word. I jump out of bed on the pretence of making a cup of tea. He's wearing a pair of running shorts. He says he's just popping down to the gym and will be about an hour. I ask him what I should wear for the quad biking. He throws me a pair of track suit bottoms, telling me it will be cold in the desert once the sun goes down. I assume they're his but when I look more closely they are small women's size. I ask him what time we'll be leaving. He says not until after lunch. He leaves and I go back to bed to try and catch up on the sleep that evaded me last night.

CHAPTER 8: Abandoned

Mid morning comes and he hasn't returned. I need to go out and buy more water. I search for the key to the apartment. It's not here. I check the door. It's unlocked. I text him to ask what time he'll be back. He doesn't reply. I go to the supermarket, taking all my valuables with me. On my return I have to ask the Security Guard to let me back into the building. He's suspicious. He wants to know which apartment I'm staying in. I ask his forgiveness but I'd rather not give him that information seeing as how the apartment isn't locked. He asks for the name of the person I'm staying with. I tell him. He checks his computer database and reports that there is no one of that name on the system. I explain that I'm over here on holiday from the UK staying with Leg who's an old friend. He says he will accompany me back to the apartment. I tell him there's no need for him to do that, I only need entry into the building. He insists very strongly that he comes with me. I feel very uncomfortable. I try to engage him in conversation, with no success. Back in the apartment, I text Leg to tell him what's happened. He doesn't reply. Two o'clock and he's still not back. I text him again to tell him I need to go and get something to eat, should I wait for him? He doesn't reply. This is getting scary. What happens if, whilst I'm out, he returns, locks up the apartment and goes back to Abu Dhabi. I realize now that he's capable of anything. But I have to eat so I venture out to the nearest café. I notice that the security guard has changed. The older, officious looking man has been replaced by a much younger version. I hope the changing of the guard is nothing to do with me. Lunch consists of a small piece of thoroughly disgusting spinach quiche and a cup of cold coffee. I should complain but I don't, my stomach is turning cartwheels and I just don't want any more hassle. I return to the apartment complex. In response to my request to be let back into the building, the security guard tells me that the nearest door has been unlocked and I can get in through there. On the fourth floor I find I need a pass key to get from this block into the next. I hang about in the hallway wondering what to do. A resident appears from nowhere; the first one I've seen since being here. He lets me through and I breathe a sigh of relief when I get back to the apartment and find it still unlocked.

With each hour that passes my anxiety increases. Without a key to the apartment I'm as confined as if he'd locked me in. I can't chance going out again. I have a bad feeling about the security guard; he's bound to be checking things out. Why isn't Leg listed as a resident? Whose apartment is this anyway? Four o'clock comes and goes, it will be dark soon. Questions are flying through my head faster than speeding bullets but none of them have an answer. Except one. Leg's absence and silence is clear; he wants me to leave. His laptop is still in the apartment. I switch it on, maybe I'll find some answers here. It asks for a password, the prompt is "occupation", even a first grader could figure that one out! I'm in on the first attempt. There are 666 emails in his inbox; it seems like a macabre coincidence. There's an email, with an erotic photo attached, from a young Filipino girl. She says he's very handsome and thanks him for paying for her to go diving last week. She hopes he was happy with the way she repaid him. There's one from another woman; this one returned to the Philippines six months ago. The email is a tirade of verbal abuse and bad language, accusing him of putting her and her young son in danger for his own selfish needs.

I find correspondence concerning his last occupation. An attachment tells me he didn't leave voluntarily, he was sacked for incompetency, negligence and "entertaining ladies in his apartment." That's when I find out it's illegal in Dubai for single people, not of the same gender, to share accommodation, even temporarily. Sexual activity is assumed even though it may not be happening. The gravity of the situation hits me like a ten ton snowball falling from a precipice. What if the security guard has alerted the police? What if that's why the entry door to the building was left unlocked? Further digging reveals that he's in the process of taking his former employer to a UK Industrial Tribunal. His defense is that all UK men do what he does, why are they picking on him? But his appeal has been thrown out and they're now chasing him for costs. His appeal letter, sent a few days before I arrived, tells them that they've made him destitute. He blames a clash of personalities for his dismissal. His Line Manager had it in for him from the start. He goes on to talk about trust and how terrible it is to tell lies and be deceitful! I marvel at his audacity and also his lack of self-knowledge; how can he accuse others of having a pebble in their eye when he's sporting a rock the size of Mont Blanc! There's an indication too that he and his brother have already settled some scores using physical violence. It's a classic case of Carl Jung's shadow-self being projected onto someone else. When a whole nation does this you get ethnic cleansing and genocide, that's how dangerous ignorance can be. It makes me question what I'm doing. Surely accessing someone's email without their permission is at least slightly reprehensible? After a few seconds contemplating this, I forgive myself on the grounds that he's left me in a dangerous and vulnerable position and I need to know what I'm dealing with. Besides this is damned interesting stuff! So, despite his boastings of wealth, he has no money. This explains his reluctance to eat out and his ducking and diving to get out of the promised sightseeing trips. If he'd told me, I would have paid for the meal at TGI Friday by way of a thank you for providing me with accommodation, but then he's not a fan of honesty. Visas are cancelled on termination of employment and so he was also facing deportation. He got round this by acquiring another visa, illegally and expensively, only a few weeks after he was fired. His CV cites a fictitious degree that cost him $3000 on the internet. Add to that a fictitious UK fire fighting qualification and, on paper, he's the best qualified Fire Fighter in the world. Shame he failed all his GCSEs.

When I next look up from the screen, it's five o'clock and darkness has descended once more. The sun won't rise again for at least fourteen hours. I download a list of reasonably priced hotels in Dubai but I'm worried that they will be used by hookers and labourers. What am I to do? I must try and keep calm. I find the website of the British Embassy in Dubai and load their telephone number into my phone. I email the number to all my friends, along with Leg's full name, address, email address and mobile telephone number. I tell them to raise the alarm if they haven't heard anything further from me by tomorrow. I try and contact Emirates airline but I can't find their telephone number; it turns out that telephone contact is reserved for Business Class passengers only. I email them requesting a change of flight. I mark it urgent and hope I can bring my flight forward a week and fly out tomorrow. I get an automated response saying my email will be answered within forty eight hours.

CHAPTER 9: Arrival Of The Uninvited

Six o'clock and still no sign of him. I can hear meowing; it sounds close by. I listen at the door. No doubt about it, it's outside in the corridor. I open the door slowly. The cat that greeted me on my first day here is sitting there, head on one side; meowing to be let in. It waits until I invite it inside and then it bounces in as if it has every right to be here. It doesn't take its eyes off me. I wonder how it managed to get through the locked front door, into the lift, up four floors and through another locked door. It seems weird but I'm grateful for its company and am happy to assign it mysterious qualities; a friend in need and all that. I give it milk, which it refuses, and some fish that I'd bought for my evening meal. I feel sick to my stomach; there's no way I can eat anything. My new friend turns his nose up at the fish as well and instead makes himself comfortable on the settee. He's purring loudly and is staring at me as though charged to protect me. I hope he doesn't have fleas. Seven o'clock brings a loud knock on the door. The cat springs up, eyes and ears on full alert. Every nerve in my body fires and for one interminable second I think it's the police. My hands are shaking. I shout through the closed door,

"Who is it?"

A man's voice answers. He says something about checking the water. I remember a joke about that, something about the plumber coming to mend your pipes. I can't even smile at the memory, I'm terrified. Is this a police reconnaissance? Is it security? What the hell's going on? He knocks again. I tell him to go away. Amazingly he does and I hear the door, that leads back into the hallway by the lift, slam shut. Then silence. As I'm engaging the security bolt on the back of the door, a call comes through on Skype. It's my friend in the Netherlands. He tells me his girlfriend has a cousin living in Dubai and they will try and contact her for advice. By now I'm a shaking, jibbering wreck who just wants to go home. I turn my attention back to Leg's computer; the only thing that helps to take my mind off this awful situation. He's joined an internet dating site for men wanting 'hot exotic women'. His inbox is full of emails from voluptuous babes with un-natural cleavages.

I then find email correspondence about two websites Leg has set up. They're websites offering "Escort Services". Chinese and Filipino hookers are paraded across the screen in partial stages of undress, crawling on their hands and knees across floors and beds; naked buttocks thrust up into the air. Google pulls up more than ten websites where he's placed advertisements. The contact telephone number on all of them is the number of his Chinese girlfriend. Oh my God; is he a pimp as well?

My mobile phone rings. It's my friend's Dubai contact. She tells me that she and her husband will be round to collect me in five minutes. They live quite close by in a rich suburb. I protest. I need to pack. She tells me there's no time and that I have no idea how dangerous this situation is. She warns me that, having alerted security to my single status, they will have no choice but to report back to the police and the apartment could be raided at any moment and I could be thrown into prison. Now I feel totally panicked. I throw all my stuff in my case whilst the cat watches from the settee.

Another knock on the door. The handle turns. The door opens a few inches; the safety bolt stops it opening fully. I position myself where I can see the door.

"We really need to talk," a middle eastern accent,

"Please let me in, or at least come to the door."

"What do you want?"

"Just to clear up a misunderstanding."

"What misunderstanding?"

"A misunderstanding about who is living in this apartment. The name you gave is not on our database."

"I don't know what's going on," I'm almost in tears, "I'm just here on holiday for two weeks."

"I'm sorry. It's not my intention to upset you. You're not in any trouble; please I just have a few questions."

"Who are you?"

"I'm the owner of this apartment block."

My case is packed. I fumble with the zip. I'm hyperventilating. I have to leave. I wheel my case over to the door, hand trembling over the safety bolt. I slip it off; I have no choice. The man enters. He doesn't look like security but nor does he look very friendly. He asks for Leg's full name. I give it. He types it into a mobile device he's carrying. He asks where Leg works. I tell him. All the while his eyes flit between his device and Leg's computer, which is still displaying the escort website. I wave my hand toward the screen,

"That's nothing to do with me. He's disappeared and left me here without a key. I was looking on his computer for a contact number and found that."

The man walks over to take a closer look, taking notes all the time. I see his hand on the mouse. The screen changes. I should protest, should stop him. He'll have access to all Leg's files and emails and anything else he cares to look at. But why should I? Do I care? No, I don't. Leg can rot in hell as far as I'm concerned.

"I have to go," I say, "Someone's picking me up,

they'll be waiting outside."

He waves his hand at me in dismissal, "No more questions," he says, "Have a pleasant trip."

I leave. The cat follows me without prompting. We walk across the hall together, into the lift, down to the ground floor and out of the door. My friend's cousin and her Italian husband are waiting for me. I feel exhausted and am trembling inside, hands shaking. My feline friend is reluctant to leave me but I shoo him away, thanking him silently for his company. I wish I could take him home with me.

CHAPTER 10: The Homecoming

I flew out of Dubai International Airport the following day. It costs me £75 to change my ticket but I would have paid ten times that. A woman, living in Perth, is in the seat next to me. She's downed enough lager to keep six people happy for the whole flight and within seconds of apparently nodding off, she has started shouting at the top of her voice.

"Luke. Luke. Come here yer little shit. Jennifer wot yer doin'? Stop it. STOP IT!?"

I wake her. She says she was dreaming, shouting at her kids back in Aussie. Well dear, I'm sure they heard you! I half expect the pilot to charge out of the cockpit and accuse me of assault. I can't decide whether she's attention seeking or is just barking mad.

Five hours later and I'm back in the UK with love and gratitude in my heart for England. I feel safe and protected for the first time in a week. I want to get down on my hands and knees and kiss the tarmac. I love my homeland. The price of petrol may be too high, there may be an increasing divide between rich and poor, we English may moan continually about the weather and the taxes we have to pay but, warts and all, I wouldn't want to live anywhere else. The UK is a beautiful, liberal, tolerant society where we can swear and make rude gestures to our heart's content. We can hug our friends in public and hold hands with our lovers. We can dance as if no one's watching, drink alcohol and smoke electronic cigarettes. We can even marry someone of the same sex if we want to, and men can cross dress without fear of reprisal. We don't refuse illegitimate babies a birth certificate, we don't stone women for being raped, and we certainly don't outlaw human affection, branding it offensive and against public decency. The UK truly is the land of the free and I can't imagine why anyone would choose to live in the Jahannam that is Dubai. I write this at a time when the world is teetering on the edge of madness. When balaclava clad terrorists, armed with Kalashnikov assault rifles, are gunning down innocent people in the name of a jealous God, affronted by satire. A world where children starve while their corrupt governments live in luxury, and where the extremist, so-called, Islamic State seems hell bent on a holy war that will annihilate everyone, even fellow Muslims, who will not bow to their barbarity. I thank my God that I live under the protective umbrella of western democracy.

On my return home a family member, who's in a safe but unhappy marriage, put a metaphorical Kalashnikov to my head and said they hoped I'd learned my lesson.

"It's a Muslim country, bang, you have to be careful, bang, they're not like us. You can't trust people, bang, you shouldn't travel alone, bang, you're stupid, bang, you're naive, bang, you should have checked things out more thoroughly, bang, you should have.... should have...... should have....... bang, bang, bang, bang."

When the bullets stopped ricocheting around inside my head, I reminded them of what Steve Jobs (founder of APPLE) said in 2005 when he addressed a group of University students,

"Stay hungry, stay foolish."

Sadly Steve died at age 56. My brother died at age 48 and my dear friend and neighbour at 62. Death stalks all of us, all of the time; every hour, every minute, every second. I choose to stay hungry; it keeps me enthusiastic about life. I choose to be foolish; my foolishness keeps me open to new opportunities and adventures. Sometimes things go wrong, not everything works out as expected, but the good times are worth the risk and I absolutely refuse to let fear constrain me. I want to experience everything life has to offer, no matter how scary, before it slips silently away into a world of care homes and stale urine.

Regrets about my trip? Yes I have a few. But then again......, unlike the song, I will mention them! I regret not pouring milk into Leg's bed and breaking raw eggs underneath his settee cushions. I regret not dropping all his clothes into the garbage shute. I regret giving the cat the raw fish instead of sewing it into his curtains. Of course, I could never have done any of those things simply because I want my last meal at The Karma Kafe to be a celebration not a punishment. And I don't want to sound holier than thou, but I suspect that the day Leg finds himself back at The Karma Kafe, will be the day that the only thing on the menu is his just desserts.

As for Dubai . . . well, it's not a place I'll be visiting again anytime soon.

KARA CLARKE

AFTERWORD

In defence of the accusations of naivety, I did learn a valuable lesson. I learned that if something looks like shit, smells like shit and feels like shit, the chances are it is shit and, if you're walking round in it, you'd better have a good pair of Wellingtons.

Hey nonny nonny.
Here endeth this sad tale of love wrong (again).

KARA CLARKE

Don't cry anymore, ladies, don't cry anymore.
Men have always been deceivers,
One foot on a ship and one on the shore.
Never devoted to anything.
So don't cry like that, just let them go
And be happy and carefree forever.
Turning all your sad sounds around
When you sing "Hey nonny nonny" instead.

Balthasar in *Much Ado About Nothing.*

Printed in Dunstable, United Kingdom